WE ARE STARVED

The Mountain West Poetry Series
Stephanie G'Schwind & Donald Revell, series editors

WE ARE STARVED

POEMS

Joshua Kryah

The Center for Literary Publishing
Colorado State University

For information about permission to reproduce
selections from this book, write to
Permissions, Center for Literary Publishing,
9105 Campus Delivery, Department of English,
Colorado State University,
Fort Collins, Colorado 80523-9105.

Printed in the United States of America.

Library of Congress Cataloging-in-Publication Data

Kryah, Joshua.
We are starved : poems / Joshua Kryah.
p. cm. -- (Mountain west poetry series)
ISBN 978-1-885635-17-4 (pbk. : alk. paper)
I. Title. II. Series.

PS3611.R885W4 2011
811'.6--dc22

2011012180

The paper used in this book meets the minimum requirements of the American
National Standard for Information Sciences-Permanence of Paper for Printed
Library Materials, ANSI Z39.48-1984.

1 2 3 4 5   15 14 13 12 11

Publication of this book was made possible by a grant from the
National Endowment for the Arts.

ART WORKS.
arts.gov

for my family, all of us

Violante
In the pantry
Gnawing at a mutton bone,
How she gnawed it,
How she clawed it,
When she felt herself alone.

—Gerard Manley Hopkins

CONTENTS

WE ARE STARVED

THE POOR KNOW THEY ARE POOR

Or we were poor and we did not know we were.

Or we were not poor and we thought we were.

Or we knew we were not poor.

Or just enough we did not deny being poor.

Or others told us we were poor and we believed we were.

Or this is what we told ourselves when we disliked others.

Or it was good to be poor among those who were not poor.

Or we had friends who were poor but did not know they were.

Or the poor were always among us.

Or we wanted nothing to do with the poor even if we were poor.

Or someone somewhere in our family had been poor.

Or it was a story we learned from our older brother who told us we were poor.

Or we told ourselves "at least we're not poor."

Or we made up things to make our lives a little less poor.

WE ARE STARVED

Always blood and those who give of it so freely.

The hemophiliac, the martyr.

The meatpacking plant at the end of the street.

Piles of ice dumped out back, soaked with the blood of deer,
        their hind legs broken, stabbed through, hung to drain.

And the children, always the children.

Gathering the ice into small handfuls, licking it as one would
        a snow cone.

We did this because we loved the deer.

We wanted, somehow, to tell it.

Our mouths full of salt and a senseless speaking.

We thought this was how you brought back the dead.

We thought you would believe us.

IT SURVIVES, A WAY OF HARMING, YOUR MOUTH

It does this
to us, to you.

All that shouting into
the night,

      until the police arrive, and then
   more shouting.

And so never again
to burden us

with its failing or fury
or you,

they took it away.

When the finch lies
trembling

on the lawn,
I bury it.

Not spared, not delivered.

My mother pulls me
close,

      you're the man of the house now. Yelling
   at my sister, threatening

animals, making
myself heard.

Does it matter
the bird

was still alive?

My promise to you
after so many times

you told me to
man up, man up.

I wear you
as a throat.

SALLIED FORTH

From you, torn things.

The stag appearing, suddenly, before the car
in the night. The car swerving.

And what she says just before, *this can't be happening,*
this isn't happening. And then the car on the side

of the road, the animal so close its breath
warm on my face.

Or is it a man?

Around us, our nakedness, the door open, the stag stumbling back up,
a crucifix hanging between its antlers

or a rosary, from the rearview mirror,
now tangled in his hair.

"Motherfucker . . ."

~

The honesty of things comes from what they most resist.

It was a man. And my sister and I drove into him.
The sound of scraping, of rasping,

of others fleeing.

The man moving his mouth in the headlights,
"Motherfucker . . . motherfucker . . ."

And later, at the station, all the boys with guns. They brought them
to the counter and left with cash.

It was called "Guns for Cash" and resembled,
in some immediate and necessary way, the transformation

of the stag into a man.

Amazing how you can move among the world's misfortune
and still consider it good.

What would they buy with all that money?

What would they do with those guns?

~

I come hither so by this hart thou huntest
I may hunt thee—

And Saint Hubert changed when he came upon the stag
with the bloodied body of Christ dangling

from its horns.

He wanted, then, to move through the world
without missing it, without making anyone else suffer.

By now, it is all a myth.

A way to make sense of it, to forgive us
the embarrassment of death and ignorance and still, this feeling,

that we should have learned something that night,
but were never really sure we did.

~

It was North St. Louis. He was a black man.

And the boys with guns were responsible, so I thought, for our
city being the most violent in America.

Some people are not redeemed.

Others simply ask for nothing.

Two kids standing over a man they thought was an animal.
The man rising, cursing, putting us back in the car

and driving us to the station.
"Motherfucker . . . motherfucker . . ."

I had seen it, I had heard.

The stag's human voice, his bodying forth.

THE LEAST CHILD

Dogs knew him.

Straggler, his clubfoot
              always strayed behind, it thrashed as he ran, it writhed.
This is what we came to believe failure to be: a boy, his affliction, what,
from the usual shape of things, broke free.

              His brother shouting above the rest of us,

run, you cripple, run!

        ~

Such untowardness.

A body made to plead,
            repeatedly, for what it had nothing to do. No remedy,
no explanation. A body in the act of becoming—what? Wastrel, more
misshapen, to us a world unbearable even to itself.

           And the dogs, how they waited.

We will take whatever we are given, we will be still.

~

Then someone calling us back.

Through side streets
                    and alleys, through backyards and lots. All the while
our embarrassment at what he was, what he carried, always, with him.
His struggle, his relentless, his still following after.

                                        The least child.

We held it toward him.

WE WILL BE FED UPON, WE WILL BE FED

Not what has
been eaten

but what eats.

The starved horse
in the meadow

near the abandoned
farmhouse.

It has almost
nothing of itself
left.

      And to feed it rotten hay would
finally end the pastoral scene.

Or animal.

Or whatever it is
that is already
dying here

in front of us.

"Coming through slaughter."

What you say
when you talk
about your past.

Who was chosen
and who was not.

Why, of your entire
family, only you
survive.

      Your mother's liver, your brother drowned
   in Alaska, the tumor found

in your father's head,
all the cousins in car accidents
and prison.

And what you say
now, when speaking
of them,

      not yet convinced, *I'm an orphan.*
And when you are

alone, stroking the horse's
forehead, feeding it

damp hay from
the ruined barn,

I hear you
whispering,

*my pain will lessen
if you eat me, my hunger too*

will abate.

LANGUOR, SUCCOR, ARDOR

To speak of Christ as a stillborn child seems, well, right.
Or so the nurse assures me.

Such a short amount of life and yet life everlasting.

And the adoration that accompanies him is one of wishing
for more—those lost days, those last days.

A single day.

Here you are.

Have another, my mother says, *when will you have another?*
And the poems about children dying, I am always

reading poems about children dying.

Like the one where Christ drowns the lords' and ladies' sons.
They deserved it. And this makes things better.

For a while, almost human.

As if we understood, finally and just this once,
one another.

~

There is so much grieving in the world.

Have you forgotten?

My neighbor tells me it is God's will. But the world is
suddener than any idea about the world.

Like the mother who kills her four newborns
and hides their remains in a closet.

Or the pit bull puppy that chews off a baby girl's toes
while her teenage parents sleep, passed out, on a futon.

Or what the doctor tells us is most likely
the result of physical trauma,

though he cannot, and does not, tell us whose.

~

Violence has changed us.

What was easy to pity is no longer.
Not them, not us.

It is enough that the pain fits exactly into the wound
it makes—that closet, those toes, the roughness between us.

And here you are, our pietà.

What some scholars have said is really Mary holding the baby
Christ, while we see an image of the future Christ.

Those lost days, those last days.

Today.

I am not afraid of you. I do not hate you.

Touch me and you touch the world, says my wife
as we cross the hospital parking lot.

And I do.

And we are.

THE BODY-HOLE

The world is what we give away.

There is no rest, only deprivation and surrender.

What keeps me awake—
                        a fetor, an effluence. Between my house
        and my neighbor's, a deadened slick.

                            Night after night, when she feels herself alone,
                 most body, the waste-bucket sloshing

onto the lawn.

That she dumps it, her shit, all summer long.

Her same sallow dress,
                    the slick as it deepens, it spreads. Whey-
          faced, how she looks from the window,

                                as if she has been seized.

What is love? What does love do?

Empty you of ever wanting it to happen again.

GHOSTMEAT

That she is departed and so
named—

      the-one-who-got-away. Blood searches
for its own pulse, grows ever hungrier

as it quickens,

what if, what if.

Like the lilac, like the thrush,
like the thing decomposing

on the bed as I watch
(the kitten succumbed

to whatever killed it)—

my own mother.

What if.

And in the morning the memory
of her

      like some meat I get the taste of, get hold of,
and will not let go. Though she walks behind me,
feeds me, sends me off to school.

What if.

This is where I live but that
is not my mother,

those hands,

that voice.

And what remains—
the kitten, the bed.

What if.

She is all the world is
when all she is

is apparitional, almost real
or just enough.

That reccurring dream.

That vanishing.

What if.

She appears the same, herself but
now someone else.

      Like the kitten that went to sleep
    and woke up dead.

It only died once.

Then again and again.

THEREFORE THAT HE MAY RAISE, THE LORD THROWS DOWN

Boys succumb.

And others, men too.

There is this danger, like that
of fallen cities.

What occupies them?

Who walks among
their ruin?

      It is here I am dying. And all the abandoned
    cities still linger heavy within me.

City of Beer.

City of Whiskey.

Where is my home?

      ~

Whatever provides
comfort, whatever

tells you that you
belong,

      the body can be withdrawn from and has.
    Getting up and walking

among us, pointing
to its side, saying,

"This I give you, this
I take away."

And the brochures, and
the meetings, and the dried-out

celebrity on smoke break,
and my own mother

when I am a child, telling
and telling.

Do not be afraid or
only a little or

for the rest of your life.

~

What did I think
that I thought it would
not matter?

There is the shiny pistol
my brother leaves

on the mantel, the way my father hurls
the cat across the room, my own

never-ending, my not
wanting it to end.

City of Blame.

City of Praise.

To already know me
as I will become or am

becoming.

I should not feel so
at home here.

THE BODY IN ITS FINAL COMMERCE

Hoarder, I take
what grieves me

from others, declare it
my own—

(your addiction, your black heroin,
your death)

> *for I loved not to suffer such things*
> *as I loved to look upon—*

(your charred-rose-of-a-name)

Whatsoever sorrow is enough
I bring to my mouth—

(your veinfire, your burned-down bloom,
your clear and never again)

> *though feigned*
> *and counterfeited—*

And unsavory.

Because.

PLAYLIST OF THE SAME

What was left and leaving gave itself over to what would come.
That moment your voice sounds so very close to the sound of what happens

or is happening. What is happening?

Close by, a cuckoo. What makes it so dumb?

The bird Ivor Gurney's fellow soldier told him about when cradling
another fallen companion.

How it made its "cuckoo, cuckoo" sound while he died.

And Gurney wanted to use it in a poem but didn't.

~

All day the cuckoo makes itself into a never-ending vowel of need.
Its calling, its recklessness.

And in the book of recorded bird songs it always sounds startled, as I press
the button again and again. As if something bad had happened.

It has that quality.

Gurney knew this and so does my friend.

They'll die, she says when talking about the soldiers, *they'll die and I'll be glad
because it means the war will end.*

Because this has already happened and is still happening.

~

Without diminution, without increase.

I know someone who knows someone who knows someone also.
Isn't this how it goes? As a sacrifice, your burnt face

gives hope to others, all the world, suddenly, larger for your being in it.
The fire was "human made" and erupted like a medieval dream

as all that was vulnerable about you came to the surface.

Now, almost a birthmark, the injury a mottling of repair
and where repair could not change it.

It is like a work of art. It is a work of art.

The part of you we try not to notice or to escape.

~

Instead, the cuckoo's recorded voice, the hand-around-its-throat call—
I want to die, I want to die. Why do you keep asking?

One day I saw you touch the skin graft like a child touching
the hide of some terrible and imagined beast.

They weigh heavy upon us, those who no longer know
the way to die. And the birds, so Gurney says,

were loath to leave their homes on the battlefield and hovered around
the dead and dying until some of them were burned,

their wings, and fell down.

~

How shall we ever listen again?

Faint-lipped, unceasing, a sound which later will seem most precious
because it was made in another country,

by someone else's hands, from a recording of a recording
of a recording.

This insipid, this nominal (which is it you will remember)—

"cuckoo, cuckoo"

LOVE LIKE UNTO WHITED SEPULCHRES

Like Saturn devouring his son.

Like Ugolino gnawing on his children's bones.

Like you and me, you and me.

Fear of abandonment followed immediately by your wanting
to call, attempt suicide, have me over for dinner, tell me I don't love you.

Where am I in all this?

When you use my hands and mouth to eat with,
swallowing yourself, your continual

likeness, *my son, my only son.*

Immoderation leads to rapture.

Like the story you tell me of the woman who pushed a car up a hill
with her children inside only to have it fall back, run over her, and catch fire.

It is what she wanted, you say, it is what I want.

CHANTICLEER

The dark
tongue of it

mouthing its way
into the world,

be the lesbian.

My stepfather
talking to me
about sex.

And afterward,
the neighbor's albino
Shar-Pei,

its awful barking,
the air fraught
with it,

be the lesbian,

be the lesbian.

And he was right.
And I was

adored and then
condemned.

Woman, I do not
know him, that man

shouting at me
as we walk hand
in hand,

be the lesbian,

be the lesbian.

What does
it mean?
Being a man

without being
one? The sacrifice
is in the idea

of abandoning
what came before,

what continues
after. And that the ending
will not be this one.

But the other
names for that kind
of dog—

Meat-Mouth,
Bone-Mouth.

What it has come
to mean, what it
has done.

NOLI ME TANGERE

Your body a carnival.

A thing we stare at long past seeing.

The drunk having wandered
                        too far onto the tracks, into the train.
            A body in the act (that moment, that shadow)

                                        of becoming not a body.

Everything on backwards or the wrong way around.

Some mangled and final thing.

His sex, unburdened,
                        there, in his lap, a part of him variegated, splayed.
            Not less, only different—

                        as leper, as severed limb, as deformity and mutilation

and disfigurement—but still we do not look away.

His betrayal and corruption, his never-to-be-used again.

I am lost as to your need of me.

We who headlong come here.

And but the beholder (that moment, that shadow) wanting.

THIS PLENTY, THIS NEVER ENOUGH

Ravaging your pear tree.

Not for hunger nor poverty,
but to do wrong,

to perish.

To want things
is a kind of sadness,
a sickness—

for had I loved the pears I stole—

But I did not and would
not eat them.

You beg me to stay.

It is harrowing
to watch. A hunger

uncontrollable
and so close to ruin.

No love
deserves the death
it has, you say.

But when I find the fruit
in the dumpster behind
your apartment,

I eat it.

There is nothing left, nothing
I will not do.

It wasn't a meal, you say,
it was my heart.

Is it good, friend?

It was foul but I loved it.

CHEAPSIDE

I hear or think I hear the cry of a people.

Not a cry—a chant, a hymn.

The howling dog chained up in the yard of an abandoned house.

The screaming of a woman being beaten or saved.

The cough and spittle of a drunk, many drunks.

They have forgotten their names.

They lay their heads anywhere.

They awake one day on my shoulder and are not relieved.

They tear me.

My people, my people.

I invent a name for them, like whistling, like snapping my fingers.

The people stare out at me from the place I had hoped to leave.

They say, *everybody.*

They say, *all of us.*

My name for them disappears and comes back to me mutilated.

My people, the people, everyone, all of us.

A PARADISE

The cries of children. My children.

Inveigh, inveigh.

Is it suffering? And whose?

The cat that moves through the house with a map of blood and matter
and discomfort inside it? The abscess

assuaged by the shunt glaring from his side, flashing
three wet spots welled up

to just a drop of blood without dropping?

My daughter running, shouting, as he sidles
up to her, *keep it away, keep it away,*

I don't want it!

~

The despair when nothing can be forced to live
but goes on living anyway,

making all that live around him aware of all that he is not—
whole, healthy, likely to live

more than one day.

To come to the moment of hope to the moment of
never-come-back. Reaching it.

Your father three months in, and what the doctors said,
and what we all thought.

And now this.

The cat dragging its slow, wounded length along, the children
fleeing his red itch.

~

How did we come to this? Did we, without meaning to,
provoke him? All those times

we wished he were gone or dead or injured beyond repair.
He is lighter than us, than he used to be.

You said you would carry him on your shoulder
and you do now that he is lost inside himself, like a shadow

or a ghost, only heavier.

You ask me who did this to him, his days forced inside,
moving from room to room, calling

in that low-bellied, sexual (how else explain it) moan.

Like words that do not get said or being said only speak
for what should not be said—

I want to die, I want to die.

~

Last night, the door open again and his fumbling his way
down the hall. Wanting out,

let me out, you fuckers, let me out.

So many times you lock the handle then break it
so he cannot escape his room.

The things he leaves behind him
on the furniture, the tile, the carpet.

Even our bed sheets, this morning, flecked with gore,
a part of him bleeding, he who had never

in your memory bled before.
Him alive, him dying.

~

Did he visit us in the night?

Did we not hear him? How did he get in?

There is so much he needs, he needs so much, and nothing
to understand it by but his crying.

The raw labor of being here, of telling us, always,
who he is.

Let us make a place of this clamor that sickness
speaks of, a paradise.

The spotting, the bleeding, the children screaming
when he tries to place his head in their laps.

Inveigh, inveigh.

You unhushable.

You selah.

MIRACLE OF THE DROWNED

I want
what I do not

possess.

I want

to give
to others

that which I cannot
possess—

       feeding upon thee—

I use you
for pity,

for wretchedness, for
suffering and sorrowing over
my own hard luck or life or, really, anything
at all.

Your levy, your stadium, your looting,
your rooftop.

Choose one.

Until, O miracle
of my empty

hands.

CORPUS CHRISTI CAROL

Your body is not.

But once bodied,
                    it suffered the same weight and hunger and humiliation.
             Your throat rose to redden the day

                                      and we moistened your lips to keep
                             the redness from leaving.

Now something has happened
to your throat.

                              ~

No body, no day.

No god breaking
              down inside you once your body went
         the way of all bodies and days.

                             An animal dies and does not know
                   its name.

So we named you.

~

immortall Road-Kill

eternall Slaughtered

Astonished
          and quietly crying, *Chris,* she said,
      (it sounded like *Christ, Christ*) is dead.

                    The cancer in your throat,
             the thing that happened.

endless Sacrifice

abiding Gone-Missing

~

Saint Basil described it this way:

An ox weeping
         at the sight of its departed yoke-mate.
     Incredulous or bridled, speechless

              or unable to apprehend or console or
       free itself.

The wrenching apart.

The wrested.

~

How I imagine you left us.

Like the bullfighter
                    we saw in Mexico, the bull's horn having
          pierced his throat and run

                                        out his mouth. *Christ,* he said when they
                    got to him, he said *Christ*

(it sounded like *Chris, Chris*)
as they hurried him from the ring,

he called your name.

MANY ARE THE RUINED CATHEDRALS OF THE HEART

After discovering
my porn habit,

I ask you
what it is like.

What is what like?

Life, this new
thing.

You couldn't understand.

Your fury, it
becomes a dwelling.

This new thing.

And love
has changed me.

Your friends call
to see how you are.

How are you?

You couldn't know, you wouldn't know.

We are on the phone
or I am right next to you,

stroking your hand,
tugging at your sleeve,

you can't, you won't.

What I remember,
incorrectly—

all the bees
vanished from

their hives, thousands
of blackbirds falling

from the sky, so many
fish floating

to the lake's surface.

I am here to tell you
about this ache.

What is that like?

You know, you have
always known.

Love has changed me.

THAT MAN TO MAN IS AN ARRANT WOLFE

As if to starve, as if starving.

Between noisy helpings you gnaw through yourself, unable
to forget the body you were born to.

I am sorry, you say as you make your way through
matter, tissue, bone, *I am sorry.*

When does it stop?

The apology for pissing yourself while on my couch.
I would like to pay you for your couch.

Not to forget, but be forgiven.

All of us moving in the shape of our own hunger.
My drunkenness, my pissing.

A remuneration.

I am sorry.

~

To keep something without owning it, not wanting it even,
is an act both horrible and affectionate.

The way my carp-like mouth, as you say you are sorry, continues
to mouth the silence out.

How formidable our failures, how wearisome.

And each just reminds us of whatever it is we have forgotten
and grown tired of

and now, indifferent.

The night I stole your truck and drove to East St. Louis
to smoke crack with a prostitute.

See?

It no longer takes imagining.

~

Bring the maimed, bring the bereft.

To seize from among us all that leads to want—body of salt,
body of sugar. This peculiar and appalling hunger.

My neighbor, who has just returned from a night in jail.

He smiles at me as he walks down the street, his mouth
blood-soaked. *I am sorry,* he says

and the complexion of mind while looking at him
is like a gash that nearly wakes the bone.

A colorlessness almost unseen
beneath all that red.

A reproval.

A humiliation.

~

He goes from house to house, rapping at windows,
crying through locks,

I am sorry, because he was too drunk last night to remember which of us he called *my nigga.*

And we turn away or do not answer.

Some of us tell him it does not matter.

But he continues down the street, his mouth the ripped-open belly of an animal on the road, dragging

its slow, rent body along.

My nigga, he says, *my nigga.*

FROM THE GOSPEL OF THE FOUNDERING

Of starving animals
you ask nothing,

you give nothing.

But so much comes, so many.

Bring them into
the world, O Lord, sire them, ten thousand
tongues, those bellies, what we find once the body has been
cut open—

       more bodies, more bellies, more tongues.

Samuel Pepys in his diary:

To Dr Williams, who did carry me
into his garden, where he hath abundance of grapes. And did show
me how a dog that he hath doth kill all the cattes that come thither to kill
his pigeons, and doth afterwards bury them.

          And doth it with so much care
that they shall be quite covered, that if but the tip of the tail hangs out,
he will take up the cat again and dig the hole deeper—
which is very strange.

And he tells me he doth believe that he hath killed above 100 cats.

THINKING ONE PLACE COULD NOT TWO BODIES BEAR

There is too much feeling or not enough.

A stone with a stone's mouth inside.

I do not know how to talk to you or I do not know how to listen.

Things often go wrong.

My grandmother this morning tells me, *we have met before.*

And we have, many times.

But every morning she is convinced it is the first.

I forgive her because she will not remember that I do.

And can again tomorrow, the day after.

Is mercy really like this?

So private, so alone.

I keep it for myself.

THE DAY WITHOUT BEFORE THIS WITHOUT

"Forget it," said Mao when declaring the end
of the campaign against sparrows.

Many thousands already dead and the locusts a multitude now
among the fields, the famine they led to, the noise

of the night which was weeping or starving or more locusts.

And we no longer look for birds.

There are no more birds.

                    ~

What this means.

A loss or a lostness.

Coming upon it during our morning walk. Such harrowing
and hurt, such a small asking, *what is it for?*

The sparrow lying in the yard for over a week now, breaking, broken.
When my daughter finds the bird's wing near the bush

and the rest of the bird with it, I tell her it is the history
of the bird, of its passing.

The pleasure of the whole thing, the half thing.

Is this how best to explain it?

                    ~

How we pinched their necks as our parents looked on, banged
pots and pans, drove them from yards, tore down

their nests, broke their eggs, devoured their young.

We were starved.

We went around making everything around us more starved.

It is not you I will miss, we sang, *it is you I will miss.*

Breaking because we could. My brother making sure they were dead
by stepping on their beaks

until they splintered.

~

Sky that empties, sky that empties.

It is our inheritance.

Men standing at the airport fence shooting songbirds
for target practice. The lime sticks my grandfather set among the garden

to catch the hummingbirds he so loved to eat. Saint Francis'
question to either the children or the swallows

they had stuffed in bags slung over their shoulders
as they made their way home,

Why did you let yourself be caught?

DARKLING

The blackbird he feeds from a pomegranate in his hand.

The red suffering it rushes to, it dies from.

Seven seeds and then their bursting forth.

My brother and I looking for another animal to somehow extinguish.

The way we recognized the ache of the world and our place within it.

That we must leave and return and leave again.

That we must sing.

Our red song.

Our always resurrection.

AN ATTRACTION TO DISTANCE AND DISAPPEARANCE

From him

what cannot be
hushed.

That deep.

That throated.

Hoarsening
             on my name, your name.
        But we are dead

in his mouth.

The way
your idiot son

holds my hand,
as if it were

his own.

The posture
of charity

is emboldening
and lurid.

One suffers.

One wants to flee.

He asks me,
          why you touching me for?
     The injured fawn I carry

from the road, knowing
it will not survive,
is one part.

Another
is the hand

of a mother
on the brow of her son.

My fawn.

My mother.

O, how I am lost.

POOR DOGSBODY, POOR DOGSBODY'S BODY
for John Travolta

Not strayed, but leashed. The service truck coming at the dogs across the

tarmac, the actor emerging from his jet, whistling, waving, the deathyelp,

the German Shepherd chasing my brother, the more than a million stray

dogs roaming the streets of Baghdad, the airline apologizing through their

spokesperson (*we regret to inform you, a matter of unfortunate circumstance,*

couldn't we just buy you another), the actor demanding something be done,

the neighborhood children shouting, I couldn't tell, at my brother or the dog,

the man telling reporters, "I wish they would kill all the dogs because they are

harmful, they carry diseases and I'm afraid for my children," the shouts that

come from among the paparazzi gathered at the Bangor airport, the actor trying,

without success, to shield their bodies, the part of his ass where the teeth had

gone through, four red wells of blood, the two shooters and two vets assigned to

either shoot or poison the dogs and then dump them on slag heaps, the reports

of the "freak accident," the actor alleging premeditation or negligence at best,

the owner pulling the German Shepherd away, crying, calling its name (*Salaam,*

Salaam), the refuse and waste strewn throughout Baghdad's streets, the dogs

that are drawn to it, the dogs already there. Not mourn, but cull.

I HAD NOT BROUGHT YOU INTO THE WORLD FOR LOVE FOR NAUGHT

Out of what darkness, the child?

Out of whose making? Because even that darkness,
though the habitation of jackals, of wolves, of boys beating the bushes

to force you into the open, is ours.

Hagar far off but not far enough away, saying, *let me not look
upon the death of my child.* That dark.

And around it, farther and farther, dusk, this gloaming, a seclusion
that forbids any entrance or departure, a distance

like that between being freed and freeing someone.

go away, daddy, go away

Because a parent is an even greater darkness.

As if I were of that world. As if, world in which nothing surrenders
but to itself, it were already mine.

Go away, says Sarah. *Go away,* says the Lord.

And we loosed the neighbor's dog into the wild because we mistook it
for a wolf or a jackal or one of those rough boys from the bushes.

Go away, says Abraham, as he forces Hagar back, away from
her home, from him.

Abandoned, or else betrayed, whatever best explains the darkness
or does not or cannot.

go away, daddy, go away

A child under every bush, the scarebabe voice, almost inaudible
and following forever us. My own son awake,

standing in the dark hallway, not moving, just there.

How unspared the world looks by dusklight,
how it seems to search for you only to turn away.

His voice as it calls out to me, a stray light that lies down
in a field and then moves on.

go away, daddy, go away

THINGS FAST TOWARD THEIR ABSENT FORMS

To clean the wound
of its wounding.

Of gravel, all the dirty
bits.

      Flesh displaced and torn
    away, flesh quickly

becoming not
flesh, the air

speckled, rosed
with it.

A little sob
everywhere,

a bleating.

Your skinned
knee, the gash

ribboning, refusing
to say

      anything other than its red.
    Your blood

at the center of
everything.

The cloth I use
to wash, the ammonia

to anoint.

Your lamb-like
cry, like that.

Only the animal,
the boy

       eventually dies. And the cloth bears
    no resemblance

to him I seek.

To lunge and grasp at,
to have, to be.

The boy running
back to his play,

faltering, tremulous,
blood-spoored.

HOMECOMING

For days that summer.

On and on it went, on and on.

We either become a part of it or it of us. There was
no telling, only the smell.

                It made its way through the house, each one
of us, our bodies, the whole of our lives.

                          We knew it, we just did not want to.

Nothing to do.

Nothing to do with it.

But we had been chosen.

               ~

At first, the slight tang of decay.

Then that foul, that unbearable.

And my stepfather had had enough.

A series of holes punched through the drywall
in search of their vanishing,

                their molder and rot. Squirrels, their young,
their small bodies having fallen between the walls,

                    their mother clawing and clawing

and clawing.

My mother also.

All of us.

~

Where are you? Where have you gone?

I ask this so often there is no other
answer—I am here.

                Can't you smell me? And the house, all the beasts
        it took in, it claimed. Own, own, own.

                            Which is it and which am I?

We carry our dwellings with us wherever we go.

We haul.

~

And the others.

Opossum, rat, bird, cat, bird.

But, mostly, the opossum.

Coming upon it that morning, its feral mouth split,
stricken.

        Its immense body crowded into the corner of the cage

set out on the back porch the night before,

its babes still clinging to its tits.

Fear and its hiss, its *don't-fuck-with-me.*

I didn't.

I left.

~

After so many years, after and after.

Still the animals, still the filth.

Dogs now, so many heads of them, baying, snapping,
shutting their mouths only when

they can eat. The frozen chicken breasts my mother
throws on the kitchen floor, my daughter's teething ring,

my hand of hello, goodbye.

Even that.

~

We bring our lairs with us.

The frothing of those hounds I keep deep inside me.

Embracing and embraced.

What fell down the wall.

What stinks up this place.

Love, O love.

CENTAUR

A fist.

Grasping and then
                    ungrasped. What it couldn't hold—the body
          now halved, now pulling away.

And the hoofbeats, how they follow me
even after our uncoupling, our going

our separate
ways.

                              ~

That night
my body

struggled
          to be loose, to be anywhere but a part of me.
      We were in each other's keeping

and each of us dragged
the other along.

Through the wounding
                    sex, its thoughtless marriage, whatever it was
          that might have been said between us.

Through and through, forcing our intolerable
weight into the world.

Into you.

~

One wants to master

what one doesn't understand. Or else
make it suffer.

Whatever lends itself
                              to wreckage or ruin or rupture. That sex is this.
            And love. Of the body, of the other.

Below, the animal flesh colored, nervous,
ready to flee.

Above, staring down at myself
as if I were a stranger,

a mistake.

NOBODY IS EVER MISSING

Fallen

into this darkened
place, this mouth, the sudden

shapelessness that speaks

of love as if it belonged
to anyone—

       come into me—

After a long
absence. Further still. Shipwrecked,
orphaned. And still further, our never
having met—

       come, come—

Saying nothing when you ask me about my day, ignoring
the children, hating them, wanting always to drink and no longer hurrying
to hide the bottles throughout the house, the weekends I start early,
the nights I never stop.

The otherness and the indifference
I have become, I am.

What if this can't go on?
What if this goes on?

Still other, still
ghosted, still.

AND NAUGHT I HAVE AND ALL THE WORLD I SEIZE UPON

We lie down like animals.

No, like a woman and an animal.

The thrusting, the calling out. Words an animal cannot understand,
only turn from or toward in search of meat.

Stay, stay.

My own hand on my thigh.

How escape this?

~

The heart, being full of blood, casts a shadow.

And so Abelard was castrated. What was once an impulse
now grown to a religion—

I must have it, I have to have it.

You tell me not to touch you in front of the children.
Not that way. And we discuss the difference

between to caress and to grope.

To grab, to seize.

To beg through life, always asking, always wanting, and never
satisfied or convinced that whatever you receive is,

itself, given willingly or with consent.

More and more.

~

Once, I smeared your menstrual blood on my face
during sex. *Stay,* I seemed to be saying,

though what I wanted was a part of you beyond
what could be offered.

Some things are forbidden, kept to prevent
boredom or surfeit or loathing.

Like the fox Abelard's parents found peering into
his crib and frightened away.

There are some things we just must not do.

Or want, or even consider.

In a letter to Heloise, "to have been eaten because now
all I ever am is starved."

~

Moving upon you with a hunger not equal to your own,
but more. Each morning when we rise

and dress for work. At night, while you are asleep. During dinner,
as we fold the laundry, the day I introduce you to my sisters.

When we conceive our first child, and after.
And after again.

What is love by any other name?

More and more.

And Abelard had his balls cut off

and entered the monastery to write long letters.

"I was not transfigured, I will never be free."

And the chased-down fox, bleeding across the snow.
It had been castrated too, and fed its testicles,

and ate them so as to breathe, so as, horribly
and without reason, to live.

WE ARE STARVED

give-it-me

Your knuckle
as the carving knife
passes

so easily through.

give-it-me

What was just before
a vessel, holding your life
as if it were—

give-it-me

                    now strayed, unrecoverable,
          all that is not ours.

give-it-me

This red.

This reddening.

give-it-me

Not-having-but-once-had—

give-it-me

          what draws itself off, what steps out
     over the self, the berth, the landing place,

what spoils the dinner meat.

give-it-me

We gather around it, unable
to tell one blood from

the other.

give-it-me

This sop.

This besotted.

give-it-me

Lining up at the table
                        as you spoon out the blood
            that has collected at the bottom

of the roast pan.

give-it-me

And our rushing toward—

give-it-me

                        As with Anticlea, when her son slaughtered
            sheep to summon Tiresias. How he beat her.

give-it-me

His own mother. Not meaning to
but doing it anyway.

give-it-me

This ravening.

This welterlight.

give-it-me

give-it-me

The fosse surrounding
each one we touch,

everything
we take.

EXTINCT ANIMALS LOOKING FOR A HOME

No animal to be found but that it once moved us to kill it.

We say they have left us.

Now children hunt each other.

And the joy of living is just that.

Quotes, the corruption of quotes, and their cannibalization from the sources below appear throughout the collection.

W. B. Yeats, *A Vision* • W. H. Auden, "In Memory of W. B. Yeats" • John Keats, "This Living Hand" • Michael Ondaatje, *Coming through Slaughter* • Sadhbh Walshe, "Killing a Dead Horse in Ireland" • "The Bitter Withy" • Cole Swensen, "The Painter Rearranges the Mirrors (1415)" • The Associated Press • Franz Kafka, *Diaries 1910–1923* • Jean Valentine, "The Drinker" • Tracy Morgan, 30 *Rock* • John Donne, "Hymn to God, My God, in My Sickness" • Augustine, *The Confessions of St. Augustine* • Ovid, "Aeneas and the Sybil of Cumae" • Samuel Pepys, *The Diary of Samuel Pepys* • Luke 22:57 • Jack Spicer, "Phonemics" • Georges Bernanos, *Diary of a Country Priest* • John Donne, "Sermon 3" • Alexander Pope, "An Essay on Criticism" • Thomas Hobbes, *De Cive* • Alcoholics Anonymous, Step Nine • A. L. Kennedy, "Internal Injuries" • Medbh McGuckian, "The Solitary Reaper" • Yu Jian, "So Hot Then," trans. John A. Crespi • Jonathan Franzen, "Emptying the Skies" • Barbara Guest, *Rocks on a Platter: Notes on Literature* • Helen MacDonald, "Taxonomy" • Genesis 16:21 • Brigit Pegeen Kelly, "Field Song" • Gaston Bachelard, *The Poetics of Space* • John Berryman, "Dream Song 29" • Sir Thomas Wyatt, "I Find No Peace" • *Gray's Anatomy* • Louise Glück, "Marathon" • Ezra Pound, "Canto 1" • Stephen Crane, *The Black Riders and Other Lines* • Peter Riley, *Excavations* • George Seferis, *Mythistorema* • Geoffrey Chaucer, "The Nun's Priest's Tale"

ACKNOWLEDGMENTS

Poems from *We Are Starved* have appeared, sometimes in different versions, in *American Poetry Review*, *Carolina Review*, *Colorado Review*, *Front Porch*, the *Iowa Review*, the *Missouri Review*, and *Pleiades*.

This book is set in Tarzana Narrow and Sabon by the Center for Literary Publishing at Colorado State University. Copyediting by Sarah Lin. Proofreading by Serena Dietze. Book design and typesetting by Lisa Feld. Cover design by Christopher Klingbeil. Printing by BookMobile.